BY REMY CHARLIP & LILIAN MOORE
PAINTINGS BY VERA B. WILLIAMS
TRICYCLE PRESS ⊛ BERKELEY, CALIFORNIA

Tricycle Press
P.O. Box 7123, Berkeley, California 94707

Library of Congress Cataloging-in-Publication Data
Charlip, Remy.
    Hooray for me! / by Remy Charlip & Lilian Moore; paintings by Vera B. Williams
        p. cm.
    Originally published: New York: Parents Magazine Press, 1975.
    Summary: Explores an individual's relationship to family, friends, and even pets.
    ISBN 1-883672-43-0
    1. Family—Juvenile literature. 2. Children—Family relationships—
Juvenile literature. 3. Self-perception—Juvenile literature. [1. Family.
2. Individuality.] I. Moore, Lilian. II. Williams, Vera B., ill. III. Title.
HQ 744.C47 1996
306.85—dc20   96–2449   CIP   AC

First Tricycle Press printing, 1996
Printed in Singapore

1 2 3 4 5 6 — 00 99 98 97 96

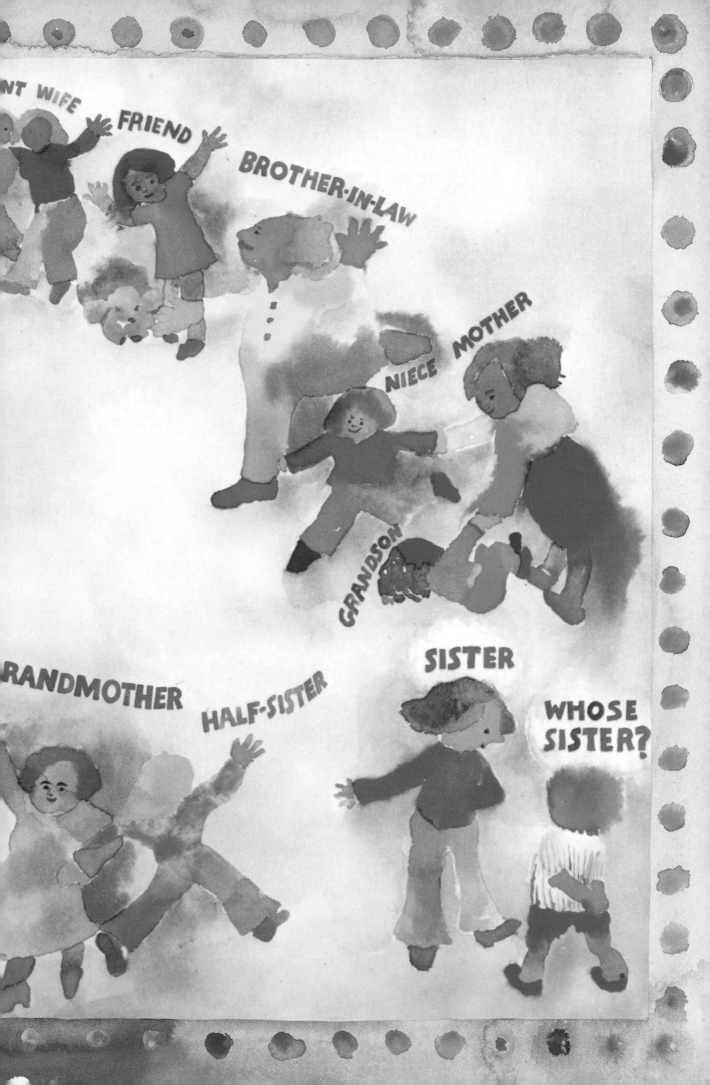

I AM MY MOTHER AND FATHER'S SON

I AM MY NIECE AND NEPHEW'S AUNT

I AM MY AUNT'S NEPHEW

I AM MY COUSIN'S COUSI

I AM MY NIECE AND NEPHEW'S UNCLE

I AM MY UNCLE'S NIECE

AM MY COUSIN'S COUSIN
WHO ARE YOU?

BEFORE I TELL YOU...

I WOULD LIKE YOU TO MEET MY MOTHER
AND FATHER AND MY GRANDMOTHERS AND
GRANDFATHERS AND MY GREAT-GRANDMOTHERS
AND GREAT-GRANDFATHERS AND MY GREAT
GREAT-GRANDMOTHERS AND GREAT-GREAT
GRANDFATHERS AND MY GREAT-GREAT-GREAT
GRANDMOTHERS AND GREAT-GREAT-GREAT
GRANDFATHERS AND MY GREAT-GREAT-GREAT
GREAT-GRANDMOTHERS AND GREAT-GREAT
GREAT-GREAT-GRANDFATHERS WHICH MAKES
ME NOT ONLY A KITTEN BUT A GRANDKITTEN
AND A GREAT-GRANDKITTEN AND A GREAT
GREAT-GRANDKITTEN AND A GREAT-GREAT
GREAT-GRANDKITTEN AND A GREAT-GREAT
GREAT-GREAT-GRANDKITTEN
ISN'T THAT GREAT?

.....THAT MEANS THAT MY MOTHER'S AND
FATHER'S MOTHERS' AND FATHERS'
MOTHERS' AND FATHERS' MOTHERS
AND FATHERS' MOTHERS' AND FATHER
MOTHERS' AND FATHERS'

GREAT

GREAT

GREAT

GREAT

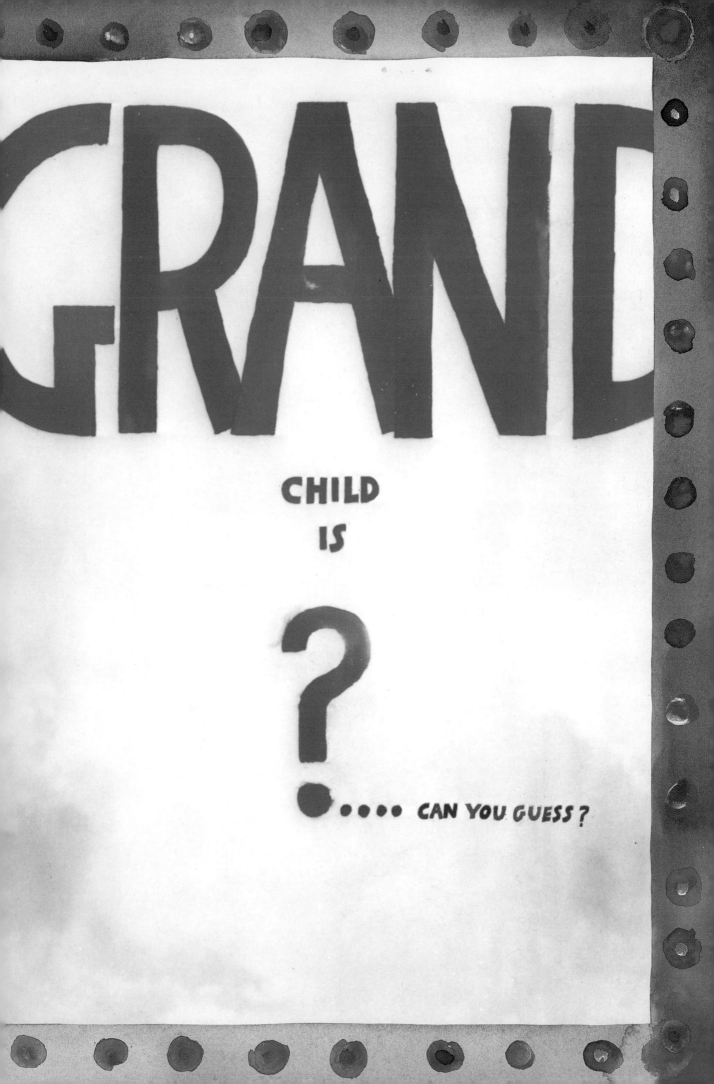

WHATEVER I WAS
WHATEVER I'LL BE
HOORAY FOR YOU!
HOORAY FOR ME!

WHATEVER YOU DO
WHATEVER YOU'LL BE
HOORAY FOR YOU!
HOORAY FOR ME!

HOORAY FOR US!
WHATEVER WE BE
HOORAY FOR YOU!
HOORAY FOR ME!